BAD PETS

BEST IN CLASS

ALLAN ZULLO

Scholastic Inc.

To my niece Cora Schroeder, who is never at a
loss for words, questions, or laughs.

—A.Z.

ISBN 978-1-338-26356-5

10 9 8 7 6 5 4 3 2 1   18 19 20 21 22

Printed in the USA   40

First printing 2018

Book design by Lizzy Yoder

CONTENTS

BAD PETS GET SCHOOLED

Whether it's a rabbit that's a classroom pet, a dog that follows her young master to campus, or a bear that saunters into the hallway, animals have always had a close—and often wacky—relationship with schools, teachers, and students.

Mammals big and small, reptiles with and without legs, and birds trained and wild have made the grade as class clowns in the world of education. This book features some of the most outrageous, funny, and strange escapades that our pets and wild animals have pulled off in classrooms, on playgrounds, or in other places where they drove students and teachers bonkers.

In the following pages, you'll find a lighthearted collection of true stories of school-related animal mischief, such as:

- The dog that chewed up the essay exams, which his master, a teacher, had brought home to grade

- The turkey that interrupted a junior high soccer match by chasing after the players

- The deer that slammed into a cross-country runner, knocking him off the course

- The snake that dropped in on a classroom—by falling through the ceiling

- The bear that crashed an elementary school's party

- The uninvited dog that hopped aboard a crowded school bus for a zany joyride

When it comes to silly animals in and around school, these critters are in a class by themselves.

TROUBLEMAKERS

SQUIRRELY PRANKSTER

When a false fire alarm went off at an elementary school, officials assumed that a student had pulled it. They questioned the kids but weren't any closer to solving the prank. Not until officials looked at video from security cameras did they unmask the culprit—a wily squirrel.

In 2010, students were evacuated after an alarm was activated inside a kitchen storeroom of Blackburn Elementary School in Ellenton, Florida. Firefighters searched the school but found no fire. Baffled officials questioned the kitchen staff, who said no one was in the area when the alarm was pulled.

Maintenance staff reviewed security camera video and discovered that a squirrel that had taken up residence in the school kitchen was responsible for the false alarm. The video showed the rascally rodent climbing five feet of plastic conduit that covered the wires of the alarm pull station. Then, after looking around to make sure no one saw him, the squirrel grabbed the lever and set off the alarm. Then he fled.

"We've had kids pull fire pull stations, but we've never had an animal do it," Todd Henson, director of maintenance and operations, told the Sarasota *Herald-Tribune.* The video was shown to North River Fire Department officials to convince them the false alarm was not the Manatee County School District's fault. If it had been the school's fault, the district would have been fined.

The furry prankster was eventually trapped by a pest-control unit. Said Henson, "It's really hard to fine a squirrel, so he got a stern lecture not to do it again and was released outside."

FOWL MOOD

To all those who were watching a soccer match between two junior high schools, it was obvious that a wild turkey thought the sport was for the birds. Not only did it interrupt the game but it also began chasing players all over the field.

During the match between Tulpehocken and Schuylkill Valley in Berks County, Pennsylvania, in 2010, three wild turkeys waddled over to the soccer complex. One of them went *cold turkey* and boldly marched onto the field in the first half, causing the refs to call a stoppage. Wanting to prove it was no chicken, the big bird began running after some of the players, who skedaddled in all directions. When a ref tried to shoo it away, it charged him. Only after it was satisfied that it had caused a major disruption did the turkey trot off the field.

Early in the second half, the same turkey returned, forcing play to stop once again. Like before, it stormed after the players, zigzagging toward forwards and then defenders until the entire field was cleared—which was all caught on video by a spectator. Players, coaches, and fans were laughing, calling for the refs to hold up a red card. One player could be heard on the video saying, "I don't like turkey."

For some reason, the strange bird took out its anger on the Tulpehocken goalie and zeroed in on him. The goalie dodged left, right, and then kept running well off the field and around the perimeter of the soccer complex with the turkey in hot pursuit. On the video, you can hear teammates shouting, "Keep running, John!" "Keep him out there and away from us!" "Take one for the team, John!"

Tiring of the chase, the turkey swaggered over to its

two winged buddies as if pleased that it had accomplished its goal of interrupting the soccer match again.

After seeing the video, which was posted on YouTube, one student said, "I was attacked by the same turkey a few days earlier at a cross-country meet there." Another viewer said the turkey could "serve as a great victory meal."

Turkeys were becoming a nuisance on the campus of the Tulpehocken School District before this incident. Students had complained that on the way to school, they were being chased by the birds. Even teachers had been targeted. "We've had some teachers come in late because the turkeys trap them in their cars," high school principal Donald Jones said at a school board meeting.

Some members of the board wondered if the Pennsylvania Game Commission could help get rid of the turkeys, but board member Scott Klopp suggested a simpler method, which he summed up with one word: "Thanksgiving."

HANGING ON FOR DEER LIFE

A deer slammed into a cross-country runner and sent him flying off the course, nearly knocking him out of the race.

Justin DeLuzio, a senior at Pennsylvania's Gwynedd Mercy University, was running in the 2016 NCAA Division III Mideast Regional Cross-Country

Championships at DeSales University in Center Valley, Pennsylvania, when he discovered that he was competing not only against other runners but also four-legged animals.

Less than a mile into the last race of his college career, DeLuzio heard a spectator shout, "Deer! Deer! Watch out for the deer!" Ten white-tailed deer were bounding across the course, which was crowded with runners from dozens of schools. The deer managed to miss hitting all the competitors—except for one.

Before DeLuzio had a chance to react, he was blindsided by Bambi. This was no little bump by a fawn. This was a pile-driving tackle by Mother Nature's equivalent of a linebacker with a full head of steam. "Someone yelled, and I caught a glimpse of the deer, and I just didn't expect it," DeLuzio told foxsports.com. "I turned to my left and, *boom*, my feet are in the air. It lifted me off the ground. It just flipped me end over end.

"I sat there in disbelief. I wasn't quite sure what had happened. Part of me was like, 'This is your last race! Get up!' Another part of me was like, 'I just got hit by a deer! Take a breath and acknowledge what just happened.'"

DeLuzio had no idea that a deer could hit that hard. After checking himself over, he figured he had suffered only a bruised hip and a sore body, not enough to stop him from racing. Waving off help from concerned race organizers, he accepted a hand from teammate Matt

French, who pulled him to his feet. French, who was also a senior, ran with him over the four remaining miles to make sure he wasn't seriously hurt.

"It was Matt's last cross-country race, too," DeLuzio said. "And he sacrificed his potential best time of the season for me. We have five guys on our team, and they were all there for me when this weird thing happened." The Gwynedd team finished 46th out of 52 schools.

DeLuzio completed the race in 31 minutes, 16 seconds, which was one of his poorest times. But at least he had a decent excuse. "There were a couple kids who came up to me after the race and said, 'Are you okay? That's such a cool story.' One said, 'I wish I got hit by a deer!'"

DeLuzio said that for the next few weeks, "I was known as the dude who got decked by a deer."

As a finance major, he said that after graduation, he wanted to work as an actuary—a job that involves using statistics to assess risks for insurance companies. Added DeLuzio, "I would definitely say there's a relatively low risk in future deer-related injuries in cross-country."

TAKE A GANDER AT THAT!

A Canada gander got his dander up after he and his mate settled on top of a storage building at White Plains High School (NY) during spring break in 2015 to await the arrival of their goslings. When the students returned to class, they discovered that the silly goose assaulted any bystander who meandered too close.

"We probably had a dozen or more attacks the first few days," high school principal Ellen Doherty told the *Journal News*. According to the article, "Students and faculty members who parked in the lot by the school auditorium were greeted by an aggressive, swooping, charging, flapping, honking, hissing bird that made sure they kept their distance from his expectant spouse. The soon-to-be mother goose mostly sits on her nest on top of the garage and waits for her eggs to hatch. The gander has apparently established a no-fly zone in the area, too, chasing away any other geese that happen by. No injuries to man or beast have been reported."

Rick Kaufmann, an art teacher, said the gander caused a *wild goose chase* when he parked in the lot the first day back from break. "I thought he was hungry or something," Kaufmann said. "The next day, he swooped down on me from the sky. I ran inside and spent most of the day laughing hysterically about it."

Senior Josh Siwek told the newspaper, "I was walking from the parking lot, and I heard this loud honking behind me. I turned around, and it was right behind me, flying toward my shoulder. My heart started pounding and I ducked. You don't realize how big they are when their wings are spread. It was definitely scary."

Siwek backed off and walked around the gander, but

said his friends teased him the whole day. "I was kind of the joke of the school until other people started getting attacked, too," he said.

After consulting with wildlife experts who said the goose, gander, and goslings could be safely relocated after the eggs hatched, school officials cordoned off the area with yellow caution tape.

During morning announcements, students were reminded not to bother the birds. Doherty, the principal, said the students were having fun with the intrusion. The kids suggested holding a naming contest and installing a "goose cam." Someone tied Angry Birds balloons to a fire hydrant near the garage. The birds' arrival became a teachable moment for those in science and journalism classes.

The geese were eventually removed after the eggs hatched four weeks later.

"Since the birds nested during the break, they probably figured this would be a nice, quiet neighborhood," said Doherty. Asked if she was worried the birds would return during the following year's mating season, Doherty replied, "By now they're probably arguing about who picked this busy location. If their marriage survives this, I'm sure they'll be looking for another spot next year."

A shifty-eyed raccoon sneaked up behind unsuspecting schoolchildren and adults, opened a woman's beach bag, took out her wallet, and tried to run away with it.

The attempted theft occurred in 2013 at Bunche Beach in Fort Myers, Florida, where kids and grown-ups had gathered to watch the release of a Kemp's ridley sea turtle named Tampa Red, which wildlife experts had nursed back to health.

Danielle Araica and her two daughters were among dozens of people who had gathered to say good-bye to the locally famous turtle as it began its return to its home waters in the Gulf of Mexico. "I wanted to have a nice experience for my children, and all this chaos happened," Araica told WZVN-TV.

She and her children were standing in the shallow water, enjoying the release of the turtle, when the raccoon crept up to her beach bag, which was resting on the shoreline. Araica turned around just in time to spot the furry bandit open up the bag and pull out her bright pink wallet. The woman began screaming at the thief and, along with the kids, charged out of the water. With the billfold in its mouth, the raccoon took off for the nearby brush.

"I saw the raccoon in my bag, so I started running like a crazy woman," Araica told the TV station. "He ran into the bushes, so I was praying he dropped my wallet."

Fortunately for Araica, the masked thief ditched the billfold in the woods, where a young boy found it and returned it to her. "My wallet has some scratches and holes on it now," the woman said, "but it's back and it's safe."

BREAKING THE CYCLE

A crazy squirrel destroyed large parts of a teacher's expensive mountain bike in broad daylight on a college campus.

Matt Strom, associate professor of mathematics at Iowa Lakes Community College in Estherville, Iowa, liked to ride his bicycle to the campus most every day. One morning in 2013, he parked his bike in the rack by his office, locked it, and walked inside. When he returned around 6 p.m., Strom was dismayed to find that the bike had been vandalized. The headlight and taillight were broken, and the front tire was flat.

After fixing the tire, he rode home and returned to campus on his bike the next day. When he went out to check on it later that afternoon, he was furious—the seat had been ripped, and the front tire was again flattened.

Upset that some brash offender would do this to his mountain bike—and during the day, no less—Strom called the Estherville Police Department. Strangely, there was no damage done to any of the bike's other parts. Only the soft materials made of plastic and rubber were destroyed. Police were mystified.

Shortly after the cops left, aviation instructor Ron Duer spied a squirrel chewing on the seat of Strom's bike. He took a photo of the nutbar gnawing on the front tire and then shooed the vandal away. "Ron Duer caught the perpetrator in the act and even got a picture," Strom wrote in an email to colleagues. "It was the meanest squirrel you have ever seen . . . Over two days of squirrel madness, I'm out two tires, a bike seat, a headlight, and taillight." (The lights had silicone buttons or rubber gaskets that the squirrel had attacked.)

In a press release issued by the college, Strom said, "I have to match wits with a squirrel—a squirrel with no regard for property or the feelings of others. My dog has been telling me for years that squirrels are bad news and can't be trusted. Now I know how right he is."

MONKEY BUSINESS

Dozens of monkeys bullied their way onto an outdoor basketball court and playground of an elementary school in China, forcing the children to stay in their classrooms while the animals entertained themselves.

Wild macaques had occasionally been spotted near the campus of Kei Tsz Primary School in Tsz Wan Shan,

13

but had never posed a threat to students. All that changed at midmorning one day in 2015 when about ten wild macaques showed up outside the school and began playing on the monkey bars (of course), the slide, and other playground equipment. Then more macaques showed up and took over the basketball court. Some played, others sat down and picked fleas out of one another's fur, and some upended trash cans in search of food. Before long, more than 50 macaques were having more fun than a barrel of monkeys.

After calling the police, school authorities shut all doors and windows to keep the students and staff safe from the invaders. Officers tried using batons and shields to scare the macaques and throw a monkey wrench into their amusement, but that effort failed. The monkeys were enjoying themselves too much.

So police summoned officials from the Agriculture, Fisheries, and Conservation Department (AFCD), who tried a different tactic. They used bananas, apples, and peanuts tied to ropes that were linked to cages. It took about two hours, but they finally lured a female monkey into the cage and captured her, according to the *Ming Pao Daily*. The caged macaque was then placed in the middle of the basketball court. Soon, an alpha male monkey ran up to the cage and tried to free her. When his attempt proved futile, the macaques panicked and fled "like bandits scurrying away after a burglar alarm," the paper reported.

A wild raccoon ran off with the cell phone of a college student who was recording the animal. The critter, who liked to hang around the campus of Bellarmine University in Louisville, Kentucky, swiped the device right in front of stunned student Guy Williams in 2016.

Moments before the crime, Williams spotted the raccoon and decided to get a close-up video of the animal, which he named Stanley. The student dropped some acorns on the grass to lure the creature closer to him and then, after turning on the phone's video camera, he placed the device on the ground.

Williams got his video, all right, but it wasn't what he expected. In the video, the raccoon went over to the cell phone, picked it up, and scampered away with it while Williams shouted, "Stanley! Stanley! Stanley!" As the student and his friend chased after the raccoon, they were laughing. The thief finally dropped the phone only after it started vibrating when someone called Williams's number.

Williams, who posted the video on Twitter, tweeted, "Had to chase it for five minutes, and I had named it Stanley like minutes before this happened, so that's why I was yelling that. I was so shook."

Someone tweeted back, "It's wearing a little bandit's mask. What did you think was going to happen?"

CHOWHOUNDS

"MY DOG ATE MY HOMEWORK"

Reggie the dog had a hunger for learning, so he ate his teenage owner's science project—a large candy-covered volcano that had taken hours and hours to make.

That was bad enough. Even worse, when he ate the volcano, Reggie also swallowed more than 50 straight pins that were used in its construction, and he ended up undergoing emergency surgery.

For her eighth grade science class in 2013, Payton Moody, 13, of Englewood, Colorado, thought it would be interesting to make a replica of the Mount Haleakala volcano in Maui, Hawaii, out of various kinds of candy.

She pinned M&M'S and other sweet treats to a large piece of foam that formed the basic shape of the volcano.

"She had chocolate as the mountain and used Twizzlers for lava coming out, with blue M&M'S for water," Payton's mother, Kara, told GoodMorningAmerica.com. "She used the pins because I didn't want the hot-glue gun around her younger brother."

Payton had worked hard on the project and was looking forward to presenting it in class. "I woke up one morning, and I came down to my desk and the volcano was just all over the floor," Payton told KCNC-TV. She quickly figured out that Reggie—the family's 2-year-old yellow Labrador retriever—had knocked the mock volcano off her desk and eaten it.

The pooch was lying on the floor, whining in discomfort. Not only had he consumed large amounts of chocolate, which is toxic to dogs, but he had scarfed down all the pins that held the candy together.

Reggie's family rushed him to the hospital, where X-rays showed the pins were in his stomach. Most of them were removed through his throat by a veterinarian who used an endoscope. Then a vet safely removed the remaining five from his belly surgically. Reggie stayed at the animal clinic for two days and made a fast recovery.

Payton found out that the classic "my dog ate my homework" excuse didn't work, even though it was true.

She had to redo the whole project. The second time, however, she made the candy-covered volcano without straight pins.

As for Reggie, "He didn't learn his lesson at all," Kara told GoodMorningAmerica.com. "[Payton] remade it with the hot-glue gun so there'd be no pins, and he still went after it."

At least Payton's second try was worth it. She received an A.

*   *   *

A woman who called herself Wendy Sheep told quora .com about her *tail* of woe that happened in 2008 when she took a college course. Recalled Wendy, "One morning the teacher asked us to hand in our homework and I said, 'I can't.' She jokingly asked, 'Did the dog eat your homework?' I said, 'No, but my pet sheep did.'

"She gave me 'the look,' rolled her eyes, and said she would fail me. I said, 'But he really did eat my homework.' I pulled out a half-eaten piece of paper and handed it to her. The whole class erupted into fits of laughter."

Wendy explained that she had left her completed homework assignment—a take-home quiz—in the living room, where her pet sheep had been watching TV. "Not thinking, I went to the kitchen to get a drink," she recalled. "I was gone only a minute and came back to see the sheep was devouring my homework. He loves paper, among other things, so I should have known better.

"The teacher accepted my half-eaten paper and passed me. After all, it's not everyone who has a pet sheep that likes to watch TV . . . and eat paper."

NICE PLAY, SHAKESPEARE!

Sloopy the yellow Labrador retriever put a new twist on the "my dog ate my homework" excuse. He gobbled students' tests that their teacher had brought home to grade.

In 1993, Dee Slosser, an English teacher at Danbury High School in Lakeside Marblehead, Ohio, came home with essay exams on Shakespeare that she had given her Advanced Placement students. She had planned to grade them over the weekend, so she set them on a downstairs bench where she always kept her school-related materials.

"I was upstairs and noticed Sloopy wasn't around," Slosser told the Port Clinton *News Herald*. "And you know, when he's not in the room with you, he's usually up to something."

Then she heard a noise downstairs that sounded like crunching paper. She hustled toward the sound and gasped. There, sitting on the floor, was her 100-pound dog, happily munching away on the tests that her students had taken just hours earlier. Pieces of chewed-up paper were scattered around him like confetti.

Seeing the look of horror on his master's face, Sloopy took off running, still with a mouthful of tests in his mouth. When Slosser finally cornered the pooch, she scolded him and made him drop the slobber-soaked shredded papers.

"I must admit I pushed the panic button," she told the newspaper. "I thought, 'What am I going to do? These kids won't want to take this test again.'"

After discovering that Sloopy had chewed up six tests, Slosser spent Sunday night piecing together the ravaged exams. "I was able to put all of them together but one," she said. "I was able to read some of hers, and the parts I couldn't read, I gave her the benefit of the doubt."

In class on Monday morning, the teacher told her students about the *testy* exchange she had with her dog. "They laughed," she recalled. "They laughed so hard one girl had tears in her eyes."

Slosser didn't stay mad at Sloopy for long. She just couldn't. "He's a character," she told the newspaper. "He's done this stuff before. He takes clothes. He goes into the neighbors' yard and takes things. What can I say? He's a retriever."

As for the exams he ate, she said, "I guess he was just trying to absorb a little Shakespeare."

Ruby the dog nearly caused her master to flunk two of his college courses because she destroyed his homework.

In 2008, Ben Parker of Barnsley, South Yorkshire, England, had been working toward a National Vocational Qualification degree in hospitality management. He had saved all his coursework in English and history on a USB memory stick. Apparently, the hours and hours of notes and essays he had put on the tiny device were quite intriguing to his 2-year-old pet boxer, Ruby. She chewed on it with *mega-bites* until it was a mangled mess.

Parker told the *Barnsley Chronicle*, "I was out at the time, and when I came home my mum said, 'You know your USB drive? What was on it?' I said, 'Everything! Why?'" Then his mother explained how the dog had ruined it.

"Ruby hadn't actually digested it, just chewed it to bits," Parker recalled. "It was up on my windowsill in my bedroom, so I don't know how she got hold of it. I was severely annoyed to say the least. I thought about finding a good taxidermist to get her stuffed," he joked. "But it's hard to stay mad at those puppy dog eyes for long."

He took the damaged stick to a computer store to see if anyone could retrieve the lost work, but they couldn't *jog its memory*, so he threw it away. That was bad enough. Even worse, when he told his instructors that his dog had eaten his homework, they weren't sympathetic. "They rolled their eyes at me and said it wasn't a valid excuse, and they wouldn't give me an extension," he told the newspaper. "I knew how it must have sounded when I told them, but it was the truth."

Parker was able to redo all his work on time but, unfortunately, it cost him the high grades he had expected. "I wasn't too bad in the exams," he said. "It was certainly the coursework where my grades let me down.

"I'm staying upbeat and thinking that, in the circumstances, I am just delighted that I passed," he told the newspaper. "I had already forgiven Ruby, so I'm not going down that road of being angry at her again."

* * *

Jacqueline Moss, of Cumberland, Maine, told NPR's *Weekend Edition* in 2012 that her Labrador retriever, Dusty, had a taste for history. When Moss was in sixth grade, she had to make a project for a class in ancient civilization. She created a brick out of flour, oats, salt, and food coloring that resembled the ones used by the Sumerians, a civilization that rose around 4000 BC in what is now Iraq.

"I left it on the radiator overnight," she recalled. "I came downstairs in the morning, and it had disappeared. And my dog, my Labrador, was looking very guilty." Fortunately for the dog, the formula Moss's teacher gave her for the Sumerian brick was more like a recipe for a huge dog biscuit. "She was fine. It must have been like what she dreamed of because it was the size of a loaf of bread, and there was nothing left."

AH-CHEW!

Sunshine the golden retriever tore apart any chance that a student would leave the country on a long-anticipated school trip—by chewing on the teen's passport.

In June 2009, Jon Meier, 17, of Eau Claire, Wisconsin, was getting ready to go with his high school Spanish class to Peru for 12 days. While he packed, Jon put his passport in the pouch of a waistband designed to be worn inside a shirt to guard against pickpockets. He placed the waistband on a table and continued preparing for the trip. Meanwhile, when no one was looking, his 1-year-old dog snatched the waistband off the table, pulled out the passport, and began gnawing on it.

Twenty minutes before Jon was set to leave home, he discovered that Sunshine had mutilated the vitally important document. "He had chewed a little bit off the corner," said John, a senior at North High School at the time. "The only thing you could not see was a few numbers. Other than that it was pretty much intact."

He didn't think it would be a problem, so he joined his fellow students on a bus that took them to Chicago's O'Hare International Airport. He showed his damaged passport to the gate agent, who cleared him for the flight to Miami, where the class was scheduled to take a connecting flight to Lima, Peru.

"In Miami, we started to board, and they wouldn't let me on," Jon told the *Leader-Telegram*. Officials explained to him that if he left the country with the damaged passport, he would have a difficult time trying to get back into the United States. No amount of pleading by his teacher could convince them otherwise, and it was too late to process a new passport. The disappointed teen took a flight back to Chicago while the rest of his classmates flew on to Peru.

Although he missed out on a trip of a lifetime, he said he wasn't angry at Sunshine because "I love her too much."

INTRUDERS

WELCOME TO THE CLASSSSSSSROOM

A snake dropped in on a classroom—literally. It fell from the ceiling and landed right next to the desk of a startled teacher.

The nonvenomous four-foot long gray rat snake (also known as a chicken snake) made its unwelcome appearance while the teacher was conducting class at Walls Elementary School in Walls, Mississippi, in 2016. And, yes, the students were somewhat *hiss-terical* at first because, well, it's not every day that a reptile plunges from the ceiling, barely missing the teacher on its way down.

People in the rural area were used to seeing snakes and other animals near the school, which is located in a field. But no one was used to seeing a snake *in* the school—especially making an entrance like that.

"They're plowing this time of year, and it makes the snakes and frogs and everything else move out of the area," John Thompson, the grandfather of a student at the school, told Memphis station WMC-TV. "I don't understand how it could have got up in the ceiling. It may have crawled into the ductwork or something."

DeSoto County Schools said it paid for pest control to spray snake repellent and search the entire school building for other snakes but didn't find any. "We can't stop nature but we can take combative actions," school district spokeswoman Katherine Nelson told WMC-TV.

FOR GOODNESS SNAKE!

A snake wanting a little *class* caused students extra schoolwork.

The four-foot-long boa constrictor slithered into a third-grade classroom at Riverside Elementary School in Princeton, New Jersey, in 2017. According to NJ.com, the students discovered the male snake curled up in a ball in the back of the room. They weren't frightened because their class pet also was a snake. Nevertheless, they were evacuated while the uninvited guest was removed and placed in a secure container by the science teacher.

School officials were at a loss to explain how the nonvenomous snake got inside the building or how long it had been there. They believed it was someone's pet from a house in the neighborhood and had escaped or was let loose to fend for itself. It made its way to the school and then into the ground-floor classroom, where the students had been taking care of a female boa constrictor named Cuddles. Officials think Cuddles's scent might have attracted the intruding reptile. The snake was turned over to the Montgomery Township animal control officer, who took it to a rescue center.

The boa actually picked the perfect place to go. The snake was in poor health and needed care. "This has been a joyous story for us," Riverside principal Valerie Ulrich told NJ.com. "Our discovery saved the snake's life."

"In all my experience as an educator, I have never, encountered this particular situation," Superintendent of Schools Stephen C. Cochrane said in a press release. "Because the kids were used to having a snake in the classroom, they were very calm."

The kids named the uninvited snake Zeus and were sad to see him go. The classroom visitor might have been a fun diversion for the students, but he brought them extra schoolwork. Their teacher, Megan Reilly, used the incident as a teachable moment and asked the students to write a fictional story from the snake's perspective, imagining where he came from and how he ended up in Riverside Elementary.

Reilly told internet news site Planet Princeton that

one student envisioned how an ugly princess was going to give Zeus as a gift to a king, but the snake escaped and made it all the way to the school to meet up with Cuddles.

OH, DEER ME!

A male deer tried to turn a college rec room into a wrecked room—and then chased a hapless student out of the building.

It all happened at the Seton Center at Mount St. Joseph University in Cincinnati in 2015. The animal crashed through a window on the main floor and skidded across the hallway. But the buck didn't stop there. After he scrambled to his feet, he kept slip-sliding here and there, trying to find a way out while students fled for safety. The deer attempted to bust through a glass door but bounced off it instead. Then the intruder dashed into the dining hall, knocking over chairs and shoving tables aside. Not finding any food that appealed to him (after all, it was a school cafeteria), he charged down the stairs toward the rec room.

Student Amanda Shelby told 12 News, "I look over and see a kid running [from] this deer, and it's jumping right over things, trying to go down the steps, but it was falling and it was banging into everything and I thought, 'Whoa, good morning!'"

Four students were playing pool in the rec room on the lower level known as the Lion's Den when they heard someone yell, "Deer! Deer! Get out of the way!" While the students darted off in different directions, the fast buck slammed into a wall, shattered an interior window, and kept running around, still seeking an escape route.

"You really don't know what to think because you're sitting inside at school playing pool and all of a sudden there's a deer staring you down from three feet away," freshman student Kenny Mitchell told FOX19. His sheer fear over the dear deer was quite clear. In a panic, Mitchell hopped over a three-foot-tall interior wall and onto a couch on the other side, hoping to *pass the buck* and avoid further confrontation. "I'm sitting there, and they all stopped screaming, so I'm thinking, 'Maybe we're okay,'" he recalled. "Then I look up, and the deer is back again."

This time, the deer was just a foot away. "The only thing I'm thinking is, 'Oh darn. Time to go.'"

Mitchell jumped off the couch, went back over the half-wall, and sprinted down a hallway. The deer jumped the short wall, too, and then bounded off an air hockey table before racing after the fleeing Mitchell. Hoping to help the deer escape, a student opened the double exit doors at the end of the hallway, which led to an outdoor loading dock.

Mitchell and the buck were neck and neck as they charged down the hall. When they reached the open doors, the deer lowered his head and shoved Mitchell aside with his antlers, sending the student tumbling five feet off the loading dock. The buck then soared through the air, made a four-point landing, and bounded off to freedom.

The incident happened during mating season, when bucks become aggressive and territorial. School officials believe the deer may have seen his reflection in the window, thought it was another deer, and attacked. When he broke through the window, he couldn't figure out how to get out.

Aside from suffering scratches and bruises and a minor concussion, Mitchell was okay. He even had a souvenir of his deer encounter. The buck had left part of his antler in Mitchell's shirt. The student planned on keeping it as a memento.

"I didn't expect to have to try to outrun a deer today," he told FOX19.

STINKER OF A GAME

A skunk that tried to join a sideline huddle during a tense high school football game played a key role in a team's heartbreaking defeat.

There has never been any love lost between the Baldwyn Bearcats and Booneville Blue Devils, two rival schools in Prentiss County, Mississippi. In 2012, the Bearcats were hoping to put an end to the Blue Devils' three-game winning streak against them. And it looked like Baldwyn just might do it, too, after going into half-time with a 27–7 lead.

But Booneville fought back in the second half and trailed by only 27–21 midway through the fourth quarter. With momentum clearly on the Blue Devils' side, the Bearcats called a timeout to regroup. They desperately wanted to hold on and avoid another loss to their archenemy.

Unfortunately for them, that's when a little stinker made a big stink.

During the timeout, a skunk ran onto the field. It reached the 20-yard line before it stopped, as if wondering which sideline to go to. Booneville coach Mike Mattox, who had seen the skunk roaming near the end zone earlier, decided he wasn't going to allow the critter on his sideline. Admitting to being superstitious and no fan of skunks, he charged out toward the critter to keep it away from his players. "I thought, 'If it sprays me or whatever, I'm kicking it to the other side if I have to,'" he told the local newspaper, the *Northeast Mississippi Daily Journal*.

The skunk didn't want anything to do with Mattox, so it turned tail and scampered toward the Baldwyn sideline, where the Bearcats were huddling around their coach. Suddenly, half the team ran to the right and the other half to the left, forming a wide, clear path for the skunk. "It was like the parting of the Red Sea over there," Mattox recalled.

"We were already in a timeout, and the skunk just started running toward us," Baldwyn senior Devonta Gates told the *Daily Journal*. "The only thing I knew was run."

Cheerleaders on the sideline screamed and bolted. Not finding any love from the boys or girls, the skunk ran under the bleachers, causing mayhem in the stands as panicked fans cleared out in fear of getting sprayed. Fortunately for them, the spurned skunk didn't resort to his famous smelly weapon.

When order was restored, the shaken Bearcats sensed that the skunk was a bad omen. It was. The Blue Devils' Andrew Lambert intercepted a pass on the Booneville 16-yard line and returned it 84 yards for the winning touchdown. Baldwyn lost, 28–27.

"I've been accused of bringing the skunk and turning it loose," Mattox told the newspaper. "I've heard from everywhere. I even had a radio station in San Diego call."

In one of his least favorite things to do, Baldwyn coach Michael Gray watched film of his team's fourth straight loss to Booneville. "The skunk was just roaming back and forth in the end zone," he told the *Daily Journal*. "It got up to the 20-yard line one time. I remember it coming right between a handful of us . . . then we commenced to getting beat."

Even though it didn't make a lot of *scents*, video of the critter's dramatic play on the field went viral, including on YouTube, ESPN, and *Good Morning America*. The game has since been dubbed the Skunk Bowl.

PAWS FOR CONCERN

A young black bear who wanted to join in the fun crashed an elementary school's squirt-gun party as well as the neighboring middle school's outdoor graduation ceremony.

On the final day of school in Bakersfield, California, in 2012, the 3-year-old 150-pound bruin was spotted running around the campus grounds of Ramon Garza Elementary School, where more than 75 fifth-graders were enjoying a squirt-gun party on the playground. According to the Los Angeles *Times*, when the bear approached the school's chain-link fence, teachers quickly herded the children inside, putting a damper on the festivities. The school was put on lockdown while a teacher alerted authorities.

Snubbed by the kids, the animal then headed next door to Sierra Middle School, where more than 600 parents were attending an outdoor graduation ceremony. The intruder drew stares, gasps, and murmurs of concern.

"The bear got on scene, there was graduation going on, and he was not an invited guest," Kim Rodriguez, of Kern County Animal Services, told the news service UPI. "He felt like he was unwelcome, so he left."

The bear climbed the fence onto the now-empty Garza playground. Because the kids hadn't returned to continue their squirt-gun party, the bruin went back over the fence and fled to a nearby apartment complex. Animal control officers cornered the animal and subdued it with a tranquilizer gun. After the bear was examined and weighed, it was transported to a large conservation area about 90 miles away and released to the wild.

BUTT-HEAD

A deer bounded onto the field of a youth soccer game, intercepted the ball—and scored a goal!

During a tournament of elementary school kids in Dickson, Tennessee, in 2015, the deer emerged from the woods, got a kick out of watching the youngsters play, and suddenly had a goal in mind because the animal was head and shoulders above the players. Spectator Sean Spidle videoed what happened next: The deer sprinted across a series of soccer fields and reached the last one just as a player kicked the ball. While running at full speed, the deer deflected the shot with its nose into the corner of the net, much to the delight of the kids and parents who watched in stunned amazement.

"This deer actually scored a goal!" Spidle wrote on his YouTube posting of the en*deer*ing score. He said the animal's goal was indeed a header.

Rather than stick around and soak up the cheers from the spectators and fans, the deer continued high-tailing it beyond the field and into the woods.

Among the comments Spidle received after posting the video on YouTube were:

- Call that deer to the National Team, and the World Cup will be a piece of cake.

- No fair. The deer has four legs to score with . . . cheater!

- The deer gets a red card for: 1. Playing without a uniform; 2. Using unapproved equipment (horns and hooves); 3. Illegally entering the field without due procedure.

BATTING AROUND

A swooping bat repeatedly interrupted a college basketball game by dive-bombing the players.

During the second half of a 2013 contest between the visiting Providence College Friars and the Marquette Golden Eagles, the bat first made its presence known with a low-level fly-by inside the Bradley Center in Milwaukee. The winged intruder then soared through the rafters and zoomed down toward the court, sending players, refs, and coaches cowering or running off.

"I think the funniest part was that the players just kept falling to the ground, trying to get away from the bat," Aaron Ledesma, a Marquette student who attended the game, told WXOW TV station in La Crosse, Wisconsin. "It was pretty entertaining."

Student Emily Fullerton told the station she might have accidentally let the bat in. "As I was entering the arena, I told a security guard some bird or bat just flew in with me, and he didn't believe me."

Everyone in the arena became believers *right off the bat* when the flying mammal first appeared with about 11 minutes left in the game and was circling over the crowd. "It was amazing and something I'd never seen before," Marquette professor Louise Cainkar told WXOW. "It went up in the rafters, down on the main floor, and circled the second level."

Play was halted when the bat dived near the court, sending referees and players scrambling. It seemed only appropriate that the *Batman* theme song began playing on the arena's loudspeaker. After a four-minute delay, the game resumed, but refs stepped in again to stop play when the bat did an encore.

At first, it appeared that the flying gate-crasher was a Marquette fan because it chased after Providence player Bryce Cotton, the Big East Conference's leading scorer, while he was dribbling up the court. Then it nearly flew into the side of the head of Providence center Sidiki Johnson, who pulled off a crowd-pleasing, body-bending maneuver straight out of the *Matrix* movies to dodge the airborne intruder.

But perhaps showing that it didn't favor one team over another, the bat then flew toward a group of players on the Marquette bench, forcing them to jump out of the way.

It continued to circle the court for the next few minutes as players and coaches tossed towels in the air, hoping to trap it or gently knock it down. That didn't work. At one point, Providence coach Ed Cooley raised his clipboard as if waiting to swat the invader out of the air, but the bat avoided him. Giving up and wanting to protect himself, Cooley put a towel on his head. So did the TV announcers.

With 7:36 left in the game, public address announcer Bob Brainerd told the crowd that officials were going to turn off the lights in an attempt to "get rid of the bat." While the arena went dark for several minutes, Whitney Houston's "I Will Always Love You" played over the sound system, prompting hundreds of fans to wave their lit mobile phones in the air as if they were at a concert.

Apparently, the bat didn't love that particular song because when the lights came back on, the batty trespasser had disappeared. Marquette went on to win the hoops *bat*-tle 81–71.

ESCAPE ARTISTS

EVERY DOG HAS ITS DAY

A bull terrier named Amaya ended up in doggy deten-
tion after sneaking onto a school bus and taking a ride
with its young passengers to a local middle school.

On a brisk winter morning in 2017, AnnDee Vorrayo,
of Vancouver, Washington, let her peppy 1-year-old
white dog outside into the family's fenced-in backyard.
She hadn't realized that a recent storm had damaged the
gate, which allowed the pooch to escape.

With this unexpected freedom, Amaya went explor-
ing, hoping to find someone young to play with. But the
only kids in the neighborhood were those waiting for
the school bus.

After the energetic canine trotted a few blocks from home, she scampered into the street and up to an Evergreen Public Schools bus that had stopped to pick up several children. When bus driver Susanne Heyman opened the door, the sly dog hopped on board. "The next thing I know, she was at the back of the bus," Heyman told *The Columbian*. "We tried to get her off the bus, but she wasn't having it."

Rather than boot the pooch and leave her running loose in the street, Heyman decided to let Amaya ride along with the students, who were thrilled to have a four-legged traveler even if she didn't pay her *fare* share. On her way to school, Heyman radioed school officials to let them know she was transporting an extra passenger—a furry stowaway—and to be prepared for the dog when the bus arrived.

Amaya enjoyed every minute of the ride, Heyman said. "She sat on a seat, facing forward, and put her paws on the seat in front of her and was riding like, 'This is where I belong,'" the driver recalled. "She was barking and making a lot of noise. She was so happy."

Heyman told the newspaper that a typically quiet bus-rider approached the driver afterward and said, "This is the best day ever!"

After the bus arrived at Shahala Middle School, Heyman carried the dog off and turned her over to a school security officer. But hanging around with grown-ups wasn't Amaya's thing. She wanted to be with the students. "She wiggled out of his arms, and ran all over the sidewalks, went in the building, and came out of the building," Heyman said.

Finally, the custodian caught Amaya and put her in a restroom, where she remained until Clark County Animal Control officer Trish Kraff showed up. Because Amaya didn't have a collar or microchip, Kraff brought her to the Humane Society for Southwest Washington.

Meanwhile, back home, the dog's masters, who were unaware that she had slipped out, kept calling for Amaya. "My husband started walking around outside and couldn't find her at all," Vorrayo told *The Columbian*. "Then we noticed the gate was completely down." The couple drove around the neighborhood, searching for her without success.

Worried that something bad had happened to Amaya, Vorrayo called animal control. To her immense relief, she was told, yes, her dog was safe and sound at the humane society facility—and, oh, one other thing: Amaya had hopped on a bus and ridden it all the way to school. "She loves kids, so it does not surprise me that she would do that," Vorrayo said.

She and her husband, Julio, and 2-year-old son, Julian, went to the humane society, where Amaya was microchipped on the spot. As soon as they returned home, they repaired the gate so the dog wouldn't escape and try to go on another joyride.

A pet pigeon named Foresta, acting as if school was a bird-brained idea, created a campus scene of feather-flying chaos.

The bird belonged to fifth-grader Tara Atkins, of Montana City, Montana, who had raised her from her days as a fledgling. Foresta liked to flit about in the backyard, but one day in 2014, she flew the coop and disappeared. Tara was heartbroken that her winged pal had vanished.

But the bird wasn't really gone. Although Foresta wasn't a homing pigeon, she seemed to know where she wanted to go—Tara's school, Central-Linc Elementary, which was 15 miles away in Helena.

The day after Foresta went missing, she showed up at the school even though she had never been there before. In fact, she had never strayed far from her home. Principal Vanessa Nasset and teacher Rob Freistadt were walking outside the school when the pigeon suddenly appeared and began harassing them. "I hear this bird flapping its wings behind us, and I start screaming, and it lands on Rob's head," Nasset told the *Independent Record*.

When the pigeon wouldn't budge at first, Nasset suspected this wasn't an ordinary bird. She acted like she was someone's pet—an ornery pet. At the time, they didn't know that she was Tara's missing bird. Before they could capture her, the pigeon took to the air and began swooping down on people, acting *plume crazy*.

"My big concern was let's get this bird contained so we don't have it going after kids," Nasset told the newspaper. "It was just sky-bombing everyone." Staff members tried luring the bird into a laundry basket, but that didn't work. A police officer was called, but really—what was he going to do? Arrest the pigeon? Taser her? He had no solution. So for nearly an hour, people were trying and failing to corner the bird.

Soon dismissal time was nearing. One of the parents who arrived to pick up her child recalled that Tara owned a pet pigeon and suggested to the principal that maybe the girl knew how to catch the flighty bird.

Tara was perplexed when she was called out of class. But the moment she spotted the problem pigeon, she knew it was Foresta by the bird's distinctive color and the blue band tied around her leg. "I was pretty happy," Tara told the newspaper.

But just as the girl was ready to catch her pigeon, the school bell rang and students poured outside, causing Foresta to go skyward. By this time, Tara's mother, Krys Holmes, who was unaware that the family's pet was at the school, arrived to pick up her daughter. "It was quite a rodeo to get Foresta to calm down enough that we could catch her," Holmes recalled.

When the pigeon landed on the head of fifth-grader Owen Cleary, the boy didn't run off. Instead, he remained still while someone slowly handed him a blanket. Then, in a split second, Owen threw the blanket over his head and captured Foresta, much to Tara's relief. After the flustered bird was brought home, she "ate like a pig," Holmes said.

The family remained mystified why the bird left the house and turned up at Tara's school.

"This pigeon has never been to town before," Holmes told the paper. "We got her as a baby, and she just hangs out at home. But pigeons are remarkable birds."

LIZARD OF OZ

Harold the classroom iguana played hooky for seven weeks after escaping from his cage.

Where he went or what he did, he wasn't telling.

The 5-year-old lizard had been a trouble-free pet in teacher Becky Linstrom's fourth-grade classroom at North Shore Elementary School in South Haven, Michigan. But during a break in the school year in 2016 when he was home with Linstrom, he slipped out of his cage, which had been accidently left unlocked. Harold took off on a grand adventure.

No one had seen the two-foot-long reptile for nearly two months when finally, neighborhood kids spotted him about four blocks from the teacher's house. But the moment a Good Samaritan tried to help him, Harold scurried across a yard and scampered up a tall tree.

People tried to reach him, but he was up too high, so someone called the South Haven Area Emergency Services for help.

In the past, firefighters had been called to rescue a cat stuck in a tree, but never an iguana. The agency dispatched a ladder truck anyway. One of the firefighters went about 50 feet up the ladder, where he spent several minutes trying to coax Harold before the reptile was plucked from a branch and brought down. Other than having lost weight and a toe, Harold looked fine.

Linstrom, who had just arrived on the scene after a neighbor alerted her to the rescue effort, was reunited with her lost lizard. Reported WWMT-TV, "Harold's owner hugged him tight and showed him off to the large crowd that had gathered to watch."

South Haven Area Emergency Services posted on its Facebook page, "It was a very emotional reunion between the owner . . . and an apparently healthy Harold, who didn't divulge where he had been. A happy ending."

Linstrom admitted that she had all but given up finding her pet and was incredibly relieved when he was rescued. "I was amazed," she said.

About a month after Harold had settled into his cage in the classroom, the two firefighters responsible for rescuing the iguana came to school for a reunion with the lizard and had their pictures taken with him. He flashed an expression that said, "*Iguana* have fun."

Brownie the classroom ball python apparently wasn't keen on school . . . and the school wasn't too keen on him after he escaped.

The nonvenomous, two-foot-long snake was the pet of a third-grade teacher at Citrus Grove Elementary School in DeLand, Florida. In 2014, the teacher brought the python to her classroom, where Brownie was kept in a glass aquarium for several weeks while students studied a science unit on reptiles. One weekend, the lid on the aquarium popped open slightly—just enough for the sneaky snake to slither out.

The following Monday, when the kids entered the classroom, they noticed that Brownie was missing. Even though she was harmless and posed no threat to anyone, school administrators immediately evacuated the entire school while searchers scoured rooms and hallways for the wayward reptile. A representative from the Florida Fish and Wildlife Conservation Commission, who happened to be at the school on an unrelated matter, helped look for Brownie. After a 45-minute search failed to turn up any sign of the snake, school officials allowed Citrus Grove's 800 students to return to their classes.

"We were searching the bookshelves and stuff," student Riley Johnson told WFTV. "We searched all over the classroom. Some kids were kind of sad that we lost the snake. Some of us aren't that scared." To be on the safe side, Riley and her fellow students were put in a different classroom for the day.

Brownie's bid for freedom was short-lived. A few days after the snake escaped, a night custodian found him in a classroom across the hall from where he was last seen. It was a good thing that Brownie wasn't *viperactive*.

FRIGHT MODE

Betty the runaway emu startled kids on their way to school by dashing helter-skelter through the center of town.

The four-foot-tall bird, which couldn't fly (maybe because she didn't know how to book a flight?), was one of two pet emus of Emma Jeffery and her family. Early one morning in 2012, Betty slipped out of her fenced area and ran loose in Barnstaple, North Devon, England. Students walking to school as well as adults heading to their jobs couldn't believe their eyes at the *emusing* sight of a big bird sprinting past them.

Some kids were late to school because they tried to help catch the aimless bird. (Couldn't you just hear it? "Honest, Ms. Smith, I'm late to class because I was chasing an emu.") Other kids watched the bizarre event unfold as two local police officers, Steve Huxtable and Zoe Parnell, tried to capture the escapee.

46

"It was the first job of the day and quite an unusual one," Huxtable told the North Devon *Gazette*. "I've dealt with deer, rabbits, cats, and dogs before, but never an emu."

The officers managed to catch the overgrown bird, but getting her into their police van wasn't easy. "Although it was quite friendly, it put up a bit of a struggle as I tried to get it into the back of the van," Huxtable said. "It didn't bite at all but kicked pretty hard and covered me in mud. People going past us were wondering why we had an emu sitting in the back of the police van."

Huxtable then had to wrestle the bird into another van belonging to the North Devon Animal Ambulance Rehoming Centre. "It took a great deal of strength to get the emu into the ambulance," said driver Diana Lewis, who had Betty checked out by a vet. Other than being panicky and flustered, the bird was healthy and hadn't hurt herself.

In a classic understatement, Parnell told the newspaper that the officers "never had training for dealing with an escaped emu." She added, "It was a bit scared and it made a mess in the car, but the owners offered to clean it up afterward. It's been the talk of the town. Everyone was taking photos."

Emma Jeffery, Betty's owner, said the first she knew that the emu had escaped was when a friend called her at her hair salon in nearby Newport and reported, "Your emu has just been arrested."

Jeffery and her family retrieved the 6-month-old bird and brought her home, where she was reunited with her brother Reg. The two had been hand raised since the day they were hatched. "Wild emus might be dangerous to people, but these have been hand reared and that is all they know," Jeffery said. "They are extremely friendly and better behaved than our dogs. They actually go out for walks with the dogs and lie down with them.

"We are not sure how she escaped. We think one of the children might have left the gate open. When Betty returned, she was quite disorientated and nervous and kept bumping into things. I think she was in shock."

So were the schoolkids who saw an emu running down the street.

NO IFS, ANDS, OR BUTTS ABOUT IT

A kid smashed his way into a school, but he was no ordinary vandal. He was a tough billy goat.

One Sunday afternoon in 2006, the goat escaped from a nearby farm and attempted to break into Hickey Elementary School in Plano, Texas. A witness reported a billy goat was ramming its head into glass windows, breaking several of them.

"At first, I thought the security officer was kidding when he told me what was happening," principal Jacque Meziere told the Plano *Star Courier*. "I thought he was talking about vandalism and not an animal."

The goat smashed out four of the eight floor-to-ceiling windows in the cafeteria and two windows in the doors of the entrance to the building. "He butted out every other window in the cafeteria," Meziere said. It was estimated that it would cost $800 to repair the damage.

Authorities believe the aggressive goat saw his reflection in the glass door, thought it was another animal, and furiously began butting it. The animal eventually broke through and went into the building. WFAA-TV reported security video showed the goat scouted out the cafeteria area before he was "arrested by animal control officers, who put him behind fences at the school district's outdoor learning center." It's not known whether the officers used *kid gloves* on the goat.

OUT ON A LIMB

Petra the Chihuahua sneaked out of the house and thought it would be fun to climb a tree. After all, how many dogs can do that? The little pooch worked her way 25 feet up a thick 75-foot-tall cypress tree when suddenly she decided this was no longer fun. In fact, it was downright scary because she had no clue how to return to the ground.

Her misadventure happened in Weldon, California, in 2015. About a third of the way up the towering tree, Petra embraced *climb-it* change. She wanted down, so she stuck her head out of the lush tree and yelped for help. Students on their way home from school looked up and were startled to see a frightened dog high in the tree. They alerted neighbors, but no one had a ladder tall enough, so they called the Kern County Fire Department and Kern County Animal Services.

Firefighters arrived on scene as *ladder day* saints. A firefighter went up the ladder and gently plucked the shaking Chihuahua, who had been clutching a branch for dear life. The firefighter brought her down safely to the cheers of the kids and neighbors. Once Petra was on the ground, an animal services officer turned her over to her worried owner.

As Dodo.com reported, "Firefighters managed to successfully strip the tree of its *bark*."

RASCALS

STEPPING OUT OF FELINE

No cat was more of a rascal on a college campus than Toff.

For more than a dozen years, the silver tabby made Carleton College, a school in Northfield, Minnesota, his personal playground. Acting as the cat's meow, Toff prowled in the library, visited classrooms, crashed trustee parties, and sneaked into dorms to take naps on students' beds—always uninvited. "Even though there was a rule that animals may not go into buildings, it didn't apply to him because he was who he was," Martha Paas, an economics professor, told the *Pioneer Press*.

Paas and her husband, Roger, a professor of German, adopted the cat when he was a stray kitten found by their daughter in 1997. They named him Toff, a British slang term for "a useless upper-class twit."

The family, which lived just off campus, tried to keep Toff inside, but at his insistence, he began staying out all night and roaming the school grounds during the day. He soon became a favorite of the students because he went wherever he wanted to go, whether it was taking a ride on an elevator in a student dorm, loitering in the entrance of the student union, or wandering unannounced into the house of a professor. Toff often took catnaps among a stack of books at the school library, on an empty chair during lectures, or on a desk in the administration building.

"An incorrigible character, he finagled his way into every building on campus, sat in on classes, visited the president, crashed a Board of Trustees reception, spent the night in various dorms with students, and occasionally set off the library motion alarm in the middle of the night," according to a Carleton College brochure.

The school newspaper, *The Carletonian*, noted in 2006, "No part of the college is off limits to Toff, not only because of his immense curiosity, but also because the campus truly is his home; Toff has nothing to be afraid of."

Martha Paas told the paper at the time that the cat "is a master of getting into wherever he wants to be." She added that one day she entered the student center "and noticed that the sea of students going in and coming out was parting around something just inside the entrance. There was Toff, happily relaxing on the floor, safe in the belief that no one would step on him."

Paas also noted that Toff, who had been microchipped, often wandered off campus to one of his favorite hangouts—a pub called the Contented Cow, about four blocks away. She said the family received a call late one night. "They told us that Toff was at the Contented Cow, ready to be picked up."

"He was quite a character," said Roger Paas. "He knew exactly what he wanted."

Throughout his life at Carleton, he became such a fixture on campus that he once got elected to the student senate as a write-in candidate, was featured in the alumni magazine and on the school's website, and even appeared on postcards sold at the student bookstore. Although he attended plenty of classes, he never earned a degree.

Toff died in 2011 of cancer. He was 14 years old. News of his death spurred an outpouring of condolences from students, alumni, and staff on the cat's Facebook page. Days later, this reply—allegedly from Toff in heaven—was posted on his page: "Hey, you guys!! Thanks for all the kind words. Just to let you know that I got here safely, and this is some cool campus! There are some awesome white birds flying around up here! I miss you, but just know that I am happy, really happy. And Pete [St. Peter] has kitty treats! Toff."

STUBBORN MULE

While Army's football players gave it their all during a game, their mascot left it all out on the field, too. But not in a good way.

In 2016, Army brought one of its mules to a home college football game against Rice. On its rear end, the mule wore a blanket emblazoned with the letter *A* and stood beyond one of the end zones throughout the first quarter as the Army Black Knights, who had enjoyed only one winning season over the previous 19 years, took a 14–7 lead.

The mule obviously wasn't impressed, because before the start of the second quarter, it sauntered out onto the field and left a smelly memento in the end zone of Michie Stadium in West Point, New York. The game was delayed while the grounds crew rushed out and cleaned up the mess.

Said *Sports Illustrated*, "The announcers were barely able to keep their composure."

Well, at least Army didn't stink up the field. The Black Knights won 31–14.

FLYING OFF COURSE

In one of the most stirring pregame rituals in college football, Auburn's war eagle flies around the stadium to the roar of fans.

In 2011 before the Auburn-Mississippi State contest, a bald eagle named Spirit took off on his pregame flight just as he had done for the previous 10 years. Only this time, he made a slight miscalculation. While soaring around Jordan-Hare Stadium, he slammed headlong into a window of a luxury suite.

Like the trouper he was, Spirit shook off the shameful moment and continued on his way. But he flew much closer than usual over the fans, causing some of them to duck in their seats.

"It looked like he hit the Plexiglas hard," Jamie Bellah, director of the Southeastern Raptor Center at Auburn, told AL.com. "I looked him over and couldn't find a bruise." Spirit was a tough old bird. He took a practice flight since the collision and seemed fine, Bellah said. Still, it was a mortifying moment. Admitted Bellah, "It doesn't look very good when you see it on the video." No, it doesn't.

DIRTY DOGS

Dogs that are college mascots often take their job as sideline howlers-in-chief seriously. Sometimes too seriously—like when they bite opposing players.

Take, for example, Smokey IX, the University of Tennessee's bluetick coonhound mascot, and Uga V, the University of Georgia's bulldog.

During pregame warm-ups at Tennessee's Neyland

Stadium in 2006, University of Alabama Crimson Tide receiver Mike McCoy leaped for a pass and then fell out of bounds right where Smokey was standing with the Volunteer cheerleaders. Wanting to let the enemy player know that invading his space was unacceptable, the 3-year-old dog lunged at McCoy and nipped him. It wasn't enough to cause serious injury to the six-foot-three, 195-pound freshman receiver, but the bite did tear a hole in his pants and break the skin.

When asked if McCoy was bitten, Alabama coach Mike Shula told reporters, "I can confirm that. I wasn't an eyewitness, but I did see that it drew blood in pre-game warm-ups."

The Smokey tradition began in 1953 when students voted for a dog named Blue Smokey, owned by Rev. Bill Brooks, to become UT's official mascot. Since then, nearly a dozen hounds have taken on the role of Smokey, wearing the orange-and-white vest and howling on the sideline.

Most were well behaved. But Smokey VII was forced into early retirement after he nipped the same UT band member during consecutive games in 1994.

Smokey IX developed his reputation as a feisty dog after the 2006 biting episode. In his final sideline appearance as a mascot, before the Tennessee-Kentucky game in 2012, Smokey couldn't contain himself. As the team entered the field for the second half, Smokey broke away from his trainer. Like any rabid Tennessee fan, he bolted straight for the nearest opponent. In this case, it was Kentucky kicker Craig McIntosh. The dog plowed right into McIntosh's kicking leg, clearly trying to help the Vols win anyway he could. (Tennessee won, 37–17.)

*   *   *

Uga V, the University of Georgia's bulldog mascot, let the sports world know that he would defend his turf even in enemy territory.

Uga came from a long line of bulldogs that represented the school. Charles Seiler, the dogs' handler for many years, said Uga IV, V, and VI were playful pooches. They each enjoyed chasing Hairy Dawg—the school's oversized human mascot—and snatching Georgia majorettes' flags as well as chewing on unattended footballs.

"If the temperature was right and they were cool and felt playful, they would run after people who ran past them," Seiler told the UGA school paper, *The Red and Black*. "Those dogs would run and chase our players if they had the chance."

Uga V once grabbed the stinger of Georgia Tech's Yellow Jacket human mascot. But the bulldog gained national fame for what he did during a 1996 football game between the visiting Georgia Bulldogs and the highly favored Auburn Tigers.

During the first quarter, Auburn's Robert Baker caught a touchdown pass in the end zone near where Uga V was sitting. While the hometown crowd cheered, Baker triumphantly waltzed toward the dog. That was bad form because he was showing a lack of respect to Georgia and its mascot. So Uga V made his move. With teeth bared, the dog lunged toward Baker. The player stopped dead in his tracks and hopped back while Seiler held on to the leash with all his might. The dog was just inches away from Baker and straining on his leash. "If Uga hadn't been stopped, he would have grabbed Baker right in the crotch, and that would have been a painful thing," Seiler told the newspaper. "Fortunately, he ran out of rope."

Auburn fans were outraged, but Georgia fans praised their mascot for sticking up for his team. ESPN named Uga V's attack as the play of the year. The following season, *Sports Illustrated* put him on the cover with the title "No. 1 Mascot." The dog even made an appearance in the movie *Midnight in the Garden of Good and Evil*. After nine years as the mascot, Uga V died in 1999.

A photo that captured the lunge has since served as a defining moment in the annual Georgia-Auburn football game, often known as "The Deep South's Oldest Rivalry." By the way, Georgia won that day, 56–49, in overtime.

SKUNK PUNK

Talk about a stinking, ungrateful critter.

One day in 2015, students on the University of Arkansas campus spotted a skunk walking in circles with a plastic cup over its face. Naturally, no one wanted to get near the animal of *di-stink-tion*, although everyone felt sorry for it.

Finally, two brave campus officers, Corporals Gabriel Golden and Chris Krodell, decided to help and warily approached the unfortunate critter, who was wandering aimlessly in the middle of the street. A student who was standing nearby videoed the attempted rescue.

"I guess if I was a brave guy, I'd just reach down there and grab it and run," one of the officers said on the video. "But I don't think I can outrun Pepé Le Pew."

Golden gave it a try anyway. He grabbed the cup, yanked it off the skunk's head, and sprinted off. Krodell dashed away, too.

So did the skunk. But first it "thanked" the officers who came to its aid—by trying to spray them, which made a whole lot of *scents* because it was upset. Golden was able to dodge the spray. But Krodell wasn't so lucky. He needed a new uniform.

ABOUT THE AUTHOR

Allan Zullo is the author of more than 120 nonfiction books on subjects ranging from sports and the supernatural to history and animals.

He has written the bestselling Bad Pets series, published by Scholastic, which includes *Bad Pets Hall of Shame*, *Bad Pets Save Christmas*, *Bad Pets Most Wanted!*, *Bad Pets on the Loose!*, and *Bad Pets: True Tales of Misbehaving Animals*. As an animal lover, he has authored such Scholastic books as *The Dog Who Saved Christmas and Other True Animal Tales*, *The Dog Who Saved Halloween and Other True Animal Tales*, *Miracle Pets: True Tales of Courage and Survival*, *Incredible Dogs and Their Incredible Tales*, *True Tales of Animal Heroes*, and *Surviving Sharks and Other Dangerous Creatures*.

He has also written Scholastic's bestselling *Ten True Tales* series, about people who have met the challenges of dangerous, sometimes life-threatening, situations. In addition, he has penned Scholastic's popular Haunted Kids series, which is filled with chilling stories based on, or inspired by, documented cases from the files of ghost hunters.

Allan, the grandfather of five and the father of two grown daughters, lives with his wife, Kathryn, near Asheville, North Carolina. To learn more about the author, visit his web site at www.allanzullo.com.